Flowing in the River
of the Spirit

VOLUME 5

Flowing
in the River
of the Spirit

*If you believe in me, come and drink! For the
Scriptures declare that rivers of living water
will flow out from within. John 7:38*

A 30-day Devotional Bible Study
for Individuals or Groups.

Dr. Larry Keefauver

Charisma
HOUSE
Books about Spirit-Led Living

FLOWING IN THE RIVER OF THE SPIRIT by Larry Keefauver

Published by Charisma House
A part of Strang Communications Company
600 Rinehart Road
Lake Mary, FL 32746

www.charismahouse.com

Printed in the United States of America

ISBN 0-88419-474-4

01 02 03 04 9 8 7 6 5 4

Contents

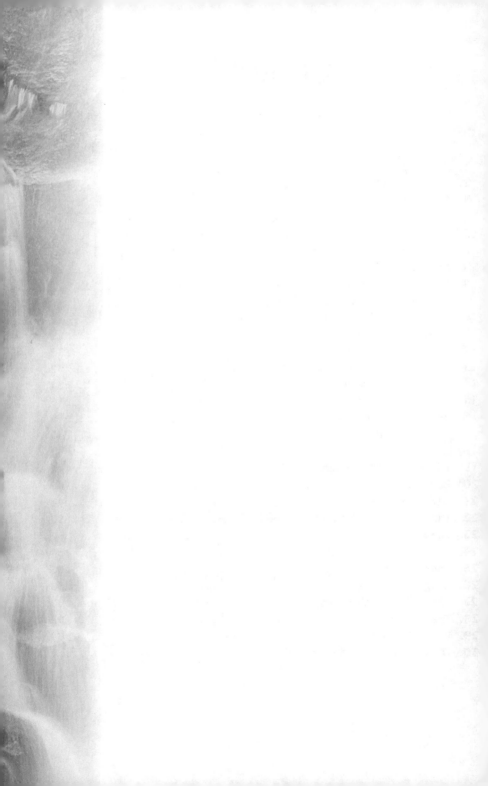

Introduction

Welcome to this devotional study guide that will assist you in welcoming the Holy Spirit into your life. This is one of eight devotional studies related to the *Holy Spirit Encounter Bible.* Though not absolutely necessary, it is recommended that you obtain a copy of the *Holy Spirit Encounter Bible* for your personal use with this study guide. We make this recommendation because the same translation used in this guide, the *New Living Translation,* is also used in the *Holy Spirit Encounter Bible.*

It is also recommended that you choose the study guides in this series in the sequence that best meets your spiritual needs. So please don't feel that you must go through them in any particular order. Each study guide has been developed for individual, group, or class use.

Additional instruction has been included at the end of this guide for those desiring to use it in class or group settings.

Because the purpose of this guide is to help readers encounter the person of the Holy Spirit through the Scriptures, individuals going through it are invited to use it for personal daily devotional reading and study. Each daily devotional is structured to:

❖ Probe deeply into the Scriptures.

❖ Examine one's own personal relationship with the Holy Spirit.

❖ Discover biblical truths about the Holy Spirit.

❖ Encounter the person of the Holy Spirit continually in one's daily walk with God.

We pray that this study guide will be an effective tool for equipping you to study God's Word and to encounter the wonderful third person of the triune God—the Holy Spirit.

*J*esus stood and shouted to the crowds, "If you are thirsty, come to me! If you believe in me, come and drink! For the Scriptures declare that rivers of living water will flow out from within" (John 7:38).

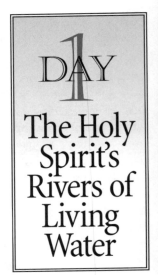

DAY 1
The Holy Spirit's Rivers of Living Water

When Jesus shouted in the Gospels, He was doing a rare and emphatic thing (John 7:28; 12:44). To interrupt a major feast day at the temple in Jerusalem by shouting to the crowds gathered there meant that Jesus had to have felt very deeply about the importance of His message. "If you are thirsty, come to me!" So coming to Him to drink from the river of the Holy Spirit was critically important to Jesus and essential for us to understand.

We can't survive spiritually without the Spirit's flow of living waters in our lives. The river of God flows into and out of the lives of believers—from the giver of the Holy Spirit—Jesus Christ. Every river has headwaters as its source. Where might we find the headwaters of God's River?

Consider the Sea of Galilee and the Dead Sea. The living, fresh water of the Sea of Galilee flows from the springs of Mt. Hermon into the Jordan River. But the Dead Sea has no flow of water through it, so it is dead.

> *Are you like the Dead Sea or the Sea of Galilee?*

How is God's spiritual river flowing within you? Put an *x* on the line where you think you are in your walk with the Spirit now:

Being refreshed in the Spirit	Stale in the Spirit

Filled with the Spirit	Dry and thirsty

Free in the Spirit	Hindering the Spirit

Overflowing with the Spirit	Stagnant in the Spirit

If anything is hindering the rivers of living water from flowing freely through and in you, what is it? Check all that apply:

- ❑ Unconfessed Sin
- ❑ Pride
- ❑ Anger toward God
- ❑ Prayerlessness
- ❑ Depression or despair
- ❑ Offended at others
- ❑ Bitterness
- ❑ Other: _____

Ask yourself . . .

❖ Am I truly in touch with the source of the river of God?

❖ Am I truly hungering and thirsting after God?

❖ What do I need to ask God to do in me to release the flow of His river?

❖ Are others refreshed by the Spirit's rivers flowing out of me?

Write a prayer asking Jesus to pour His living waters through your life from the rivers of the Holy Spirit:

_____

_____

_____

*T*he water I give them takes away thirst altogether. It becomes a perpetual spring within them, giving them eternal life (John 4:13–14).

Everything in this world eventually runs out. But there is a fountain that never runs dry. Look at the list below and circle those things that are eternal. Then underline those things that will expire.

DAY 2
The Perpetual Spring

Money	Time	
Happiness	Love	
Joy	Peace	
Freedom	The Spirit	Relationships
Holiness	Truth	Possessions

Jesus was filled and overflowing with the Spirit of God. "For he is sent by God. He speaks God's words, for God's Spirit is upon him without measure or limit" (John 3:34). And that same limitless Spirit fills and overflows you with His power and presence.

But sometimes we become dry and thirsty in our lives because we somehow get cut off from the river of God. The spring of His Spirit perpetually flows from the throne of God into our hearts. The flow of the Holy Spirit into our lives is increased or decreased by turning on certain Holy Spirit "faucets" to their maximum level.

It is up to you to control the volume of the power and blessing of His Spirit that springs from your heart into every aspect of your life. Below are some faucets that will increase the flow of His perpetual spring within you. Put an *x* on each line to indicate the flow of the Spirit in that area of your life right now.

Bible Study

Shut off	Steady Flow	Overflowing

Prayer

Shut off	Steady Flow	Overflowing

Praise and Worship

Shut off	Steady Flow	Overflowing

Serving

Shut off	Steady Flow	Overflowing

Giving

Shut off	Steady Flow	Overflowing

Witnessing

Shut off	Steady Flow	Overflowing

When we fully release Jesus to live in and through us, the Spirit flows freely from us into the lives of those we love and serve.

Ask yourself . . .

❖ Are you allowing the perpetual spring of God's Spirit to flow freely in your life?

❖ What will increase the flow?

❖ What worldly things are making you thirsty that you need to abandon?

Write a prayer telling the Lord what you will do to increase the flow of His Spirit within you:

_____

_____

_____

_____

_____

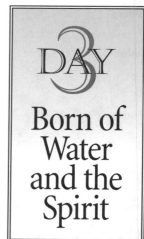

*J*esus replied, "The truth is, no one can enter the Kingdom of God without being born of water and the Spirit *(John 3:5).*

Being born of water and the Spirit points to the truth of water baptism and the spiritual reality of the new birth of God's Holy Spirit. In the natural, water baptism represents many things that happen in the supernatural.

The following passages describe what it means to be born of water. Read each passage carefully and jot down what baptism means according to God's word:

Matthew 3:6–16 _____

_____

Acts 2:38 _____

Acts 10:44–48 _____

Acts 19:1–5 _____

Romans 6:1–4 _____

1 Corinthians 12:13 _____

Galatians 3:27 _____

Ephesians 5:26 _____

Colossians 2:12_____

1 Peter 3:21 _____

A person's new birth through the water and the Spirit marks the beginning of his or her Christian life. The Holy Spirit's work of regeneration makes us new creations in Christ Jesus (2 Cor. 5:17). And there is new and eternal life in the river of God (Rev. 22:1–2).

> *The river of God's Spirit births new life in us, and continues to birth God's fresh, new work every day.*

Once saved by faith in Christ, the born-again believer flows in the river of God's Holy Spirit, who renews, refreshes, sanctifies, baptizes, anoints, and fills the believer from the day of conversion until the day the believer joins Jesus for eternity.

We need cleansing every day to wash away the old and refresh us with the new. The washing of God's Spirit flushes away sin through the shed blood of Christ. And confession opens the floodgates of God's river into our lives. "But if we confess our sins to him, he is faithful and just to forgive us and to cleanse us from every wrong" (1 John 1:9). So open the floodgates now by completing the following sentence:

Jesus, I confess that _____

_____.

Ask yourself . . .

❖ Have you been asking for cleansing in God's river?

❖ How has the Holy Spirit been working through you since you have been born of water and the Spirit?

❖ What gifts of grace from His Spirit are you thankful for in your life now that you know Jesus?

Write a prayer thanking the Lord for giving you a new birth in water and the Spirit:

_____

_____

_____

_____

_____

A nd the angel showed me a pure river with the water of life, clear as crystal, flowing from the throne of God and of the Lamb, coursing down the center of the main street (Rev. 22:1–2).

DAY 4

The River of Life

The perpetual stream of the Spirit within you gushes from the very throne room of God where Jesus sits on the right hand of God making intercession for you (Isa. 53:12; Heb. 8–10).

Fed by the river of God, you are a tree that bears fruit through the power of God's Spirit. Read each of the following scriptures, and name the fruit that your tree bears because you are watered by the river of God's Holy Spirit:

Psalm 1 _____

Psalm 52:8 _____

Psalm 92:12 _____

Psalm 128:3 _____

Proverbs 3:18 _____

Proverbs 11:30 _____

Jeremiah 17:7–8 _____

Ezekiel 47:1–12 _____

Matthew 7:16–17 _____

Romans 11:16–17 _____

The river of God's Holy Spirit brings His fullness of life into our daily existence. Without His river, we merely exist. But in the river, we live and flourish abundantly. Read John 10:10, then complete these sentences:

Abundant life in Christ is _____

_____.

Existing without Christ was _____

_____.

Now read Psalms 103:1–5, and put an *x* on each line to indicate how abundantly you are experiencing the flowing life of God's Spirit within you:

"He forgives all my sins . . ."   _____

                                        Lack   Abundant

14

" . . .and heals all my diseases."

Lack   Abundant

"He ransoms me from death . . ."

Lack   Abundant

" . . .and surrounds me with love and tender mercies."

Lack   Abundant

"He fills my life with good things."

Lack   Abundant

"My youth is renewed like the eagle's!"

Lack   Abundant

> *Rooted in the river of God's Spirit, we flourish like a tree bearing good fruit and enjoying life.*

Ask yourself . . .

❖ What good fruit is being produced in your life by the Holy Spirit?

❖ Where is the lack of your life?

❖ Will you allow the river of God to wash away all lack in your life—spiritual, emotional, mental, or physical?

Write a prayer inviting the Holy Spirit to produce abundant fruit in your life:

_____

_____

_____

_____

_____

*N*ow *turn from your sins and turn to God, so you can be cleansed of your sins. Then wonderful times of refreshing will come to you from the presence of the Lord, and He will send Jesus your Messiah to you again (Acts 3:19–20).*

Have you ever been on a long road trip and become very dry and thirsty? Then a roadside sign suddenly announced an upcoming place that had refreshments! And before you ever arrived at the place of refreshing you could almost taste a cold drink.

The wilderness of sin produces parching dryness and unquenchable thirst in us that there is no refreshment for, except the Holy Spirit. Circle everything below that you have experienced in your desert of sin:

Depression	Hopelessness
Despair	Thirst for God
Pain	Hurt
Bitterness	Anger
Guilt	Other: _____

The only exit available from sin's wasteland is repentance. And the only way to open your heart to the flow of God's river is to turn *from* sin and *to* Christ as your Savior and Lord. Read the following scriptures and jot down what you must do to repent:

1 Kings 8:47–51 _____

2 Kings 22:19 _____

2 Chronicles 34:27 _____

Lamentations 3:40 _____

Luke 24:47 _____

Acts 2:38 _____

2 Peter 3:9 _____

> *Repentance opens the floodgates of God's refreshing waters that flood the parched wastelands of our soul. Humility restores life where death once reigned.*

Consider any offense you still hold onto, or any sin that you still harbor, then repent of anything the Holy Spirit's conviction inspires in your heart.

Ask yourself . . .

❖ What do you need to repent of from the past?

❖ In what ways are you experiencing the Spirit's refreshing?

❖ What deserts in your soul need refreshing now?

Write a prayer of repentance asking for the refreshing river of God to flood through you:

_____

_____

_____

_____

_____

*T*hen the man brought me back to the entrance of the Temple. There I saw a stream flowing eastward from beneath the Temple threshold. This stream them passed to the right of the altar on its south side (Ezek. 47:1–2).

At the center of Ezekiel's prophetic temple is the holy of holies—the place where the Spirit of God dwells within the ark of the covenant. Ezekiel prophetically declares that the Spirit of God would flow out from the temple and touch God's people.

First, people would be touched by the stream of God's Spirit on their ankles—representing their walk in the spirit. Then the stream would rise to their knees—representative of praying in the Spirit. The stream would then rise to their waists—representing the girding up of one's loins to work and serve. Then, finally, the river would rise above a believer's head, so deep in fact, that one could only swim (47:5). The deep waters represent the baptism in the Holy Spirit.

Remember: God desires to flood every area of our lives with the river of His Spirit. His river brings healing and power into our lives. Read Ezekiel 47:6–10 and summarize in your own words what the river does in your life:

_____

_____

The river of God is a stream of holiness that flows from the temple's holy of holies. To be *holy* means to *be set apart and consecrated to the Lord*. The work of sanctification in the Holy Spirit is His process of making us pure and holy unto the Lord.

Read the following passages that speak about the Spirit's processes that make us holy in His river. Then jot down what each passage says about how His Spirit is working in your life to make *you* holy:

John 17:17–19_____

1 Corinthians 1:30 _____

Ephesians 5:26 _____

1 Thessalonians 4:3–4 _____

1 Thessalonians 5:23 _____

2 Thessalonians 2:13 _____

Hebrews 13:12 _____

1 Peter 1:2 _____

Let the river of God flow out of the holy of holies into your life to purify, cleanse, and set you apart for His purpose.

> *Don't settle for simply wading in God's river. Go swimming! Be immersed in the deep waters of the Holy Spirit's river of sanctification.*

Ask yourself . . .

❖ How deep is the river in your life?

❖ In what ways is the Holy Spirit sanctifying you?

Write a prayer asking God's Spirit to sanctify you as He washes you in His river:

_____

_____

_____

_____

_____

DAY 7

Hunger and Thirst

*Y*ou sent your good Spirit to instruct them, and you did not stop giving them bread from heaven or water for their thirst (Neh. 9:20).

What are you hungry and thirsty for from God's Spirit? Bread represents the living Word of God. Water represents the river of His Spirit.

Hunger and thirst on our part don't indicate a lack of willingness to give on God's part. But they do indicate a deep and abiding need within us that can never be fully satisfied. When we become satisfied with the Word of God, we become stale and religious in our spiritual walk. When we become satisfied with the river of God, we become stagnant and comfortably pious in our desire to spiritually grow.

> *The more we feed on God's Word, the more we hunger for more! The greater our thirst for His Spirit, the deeper we will desire to plunge into His flow.*

Lack of hunger and thirst within us produces hypocrisy. Hypocrites go through the motions of religious ritual without having an abiding, deep intimacy with the Holy Spirit. 2 Timothy 3:1–9 describes the characteristics of this kind of "form of godliness" or *religious acting*. Read this passage, and take some prayerful time to prioritize the following characteristics that you have observed in the church today from 1 (most prevalent), to 17 (least prevalent).

_____ Selfishness and self-centeredness

_____ Arrogance and pride

_____ Love of money

_____ Boastfulness

_____ Scoffing at and mocking God

_____ Disobeying and rebelling against parents

_____ An attitude of ingratitude

_____ No awe or reverence for the things of God

_____ Unloving and unforgiving

_____ Slander and gossip

_____ Lack of self-control

_____ Cruelty and abuse toward others

_____ No interest in what is good

_____ Betraying friends

_____ Recklessness and foolishness

_____ Loving pleasure more than God

_____ False teaching

Now, in an honest self-examination, circle any qualities on this list that you have noticed in yourself.

Ask yourself . . .

❖ Do you hunger for His bread and thirst for His water more and more every day?

❖ How can you become more yielded to a deeper work of His Spirit in your life:

Write a prayer asking God to increase your hunger for the bread of His Word and thirst for His Spirit:

_____

_____

_____

_____

_____

P *urify me from my sins, and I will be clean; wash me, and I will be whiter than snow. . .Create in me a clean heart, O God. Renew a right spirit within me (Ps. 51:7, 10).*

Purified and Cleansed

God's river purifies and cleanses us from sin. Without the continual flow of His Spirit into our lives, we would be increasingly burdened with sin and impurities.

Just as natural water purifies and cleanses our natural bodies, so the fountains of God's supernatural living water (the Holy Spirit) cleanse and purify us spiritually. List the purifying qualities of His cleansing power as requested by the psalmist in Psalm 51:

51:7 _____

51:8 _____

51:9 _____

51:10 _____

51:11 _____

51:12 _____

51:13 _____

51:14 _____

51:15 _____

Now notice in Psalm 51 the purifying actions that will flow *out* of our lives because of the Holy Spirit's flow *into* our lives. Here is a list of some of those actions. Check those that are happening right now in your life and circle those you want to see happen.

❑ Rejoicing	❑ Renewing	❑ Restoring
❑ Cleaning	❑ Purifying	❑ Teaching
❑ Singing	❑ Forgiving	❑ Praising
❑ Worshiping	❑ Confessing	❑ Repenting

These works of the Holy Spirit flowing in, through, and out of us, don't happen once. They happen continually.

> *We not only give witness to what the Holy Spirit has done and pray for what He will do in us, we also encounter Him moment to moment as His river perpetually flows within us.*

Read these passages about purity: Romans 15:16; 2 Timothy 2:21–22; James 5:17. Then complete the following sentences:

1. When I am purified by the river, I become _____
_____to God.

2. A pure believer can be used by God like _____
_____.

3. Pure wisdom from heaven is _____
_____.

The flow of God's river within us cleanses and purifies us as we open the floodgates of confession (1 John 1:9). Unconfessed sin becomes a dam that can stop God's river, stagnate our lives with impurities, and render us powerless to minister in the boldness, gifts, signs, and wonders of the Spirit.

Ask yourself . . .

❖ Is there unconfessed sin and a lack of repentance in your life that keeps you impure and unclean? If so, what is it?

❖ What actions resulting from the flow of God's river need to increase in your life?

Write a prayer of repentance and confession asking the Holy Spirit to cleanse and purify you:

_____

_____

_____

_____

_____

U ntil at last the Spirit is poured down upon us from heaven. . .Justice will rule in the wilderness and righteousness in the fertile field (Isa. 32:15–16).

Poured From Heaven

The river of God produces justice and righteousness in our lives, and in our land. Justice (*mishpat*) is correct and truthful judgment. So one who is just treats others with honor and dignity in lawful accordance with God's Word.

The river of God poured out from heaven produces His justice in our lives to give us His ability to love others as He loves us. Lives and lands without justice don't have the river of God flowing through them. Justice springs out of righteousness (*tsedaqah*). And righteousness establishes right relationship between ourselves and God that flows to those around us. It is the Spirit of God who produces a hunger and thirst for justice and righteousness in our lives (Matt. 5:6). So for us to be just and righteous, we must surrender all to Him.

Matthew 6 describes how we can appropriate God's righteousness and justice in our daily lives. Below is a treasure chest. On it, list all the earthly possessions you regard as precious and important to you:

Now circle all the items in your treasure chest that you have completely surrendered to God's Spirit. Write a prayer surrendering those you have not circled:

_____

_____

_____

As the river of God's Spirit is poured out from heaven, the Lord's justice and righteousness flow through our lives and into our land. Then peace, quietness, and confidence fill and overflow us (Isa. 32:17). One measure of the intensity and volume of God's flow from heaven is the Spirit's level of peace, quietness, and confidence we encounter in life. Write a brief description of how each of these qualities (peace, confidence, and quietness) are operating in your life:

_____

_____

_____

Ask yourself . . .

❖ In what ways do justice and righteousness flow from your life?

❖ What would increase peace, confidence, and quietness in your life?

Write a prayer asking God's Spirit to increase and pour out His river of righteousness and justice in your life:

_____

_____

_____

_____

_____

*B*ut now, listen to me, Jacob my servant, Israel my chosen one. The Lord who made you and helps you says. . .I will give you abundant water to quench your thirst and to moisten your parched fields (Isa. 44:2–3).

Both spiritual and physical blessings flow as God's Spirit is poured out upon us and our children. Children, in a sense, are parent's tenderly cultivated fields.

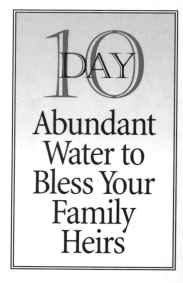

Abundant Water to Bless Your Family Heirs

Godly parents long to see their children blessed (Luke 11:11–13). And God's Word instructs us as good parents to leave an inheritance for future generations (Prov. 13:22).

What inheritance are you planning to leave your children and grandchildren? Check all you intend to leave:

❑ Land   ❑ Money   ❑ Investments

❑ Property   ❑ House(s)   ❑ Furniture

❑ Knowledge of God   ❑ Spiritual wisdom   ❑ A house of worship

❑ A Bible school   ❑ Other:_____

List some of the blessings you have received that you wish to pass on to your children and grandchildren:

1._____

2._____

3._____

4._____

5._____

Now read Exodus 20:4–6 and Deuteronomy 28. What curses do you want to see broken by the Spirit in your life so they won't be passed on to the third and fourth generations? Write a prayer asking God's Spirit to break any curse in your life through His anointing and the blood of Christ.

_____

_____

_____

_____

The river of God poured out into your children's lives will continue to meet their needs long after you pass on into glory. Are you leaving your children an inheritance that will last forever?

Ask yourself . . .

❖ What inheritance are you leaving your children?

❖ What bondage do you presently have that needs to be broken by the Spirit so your children can be free?

Write a prayer asking God to pour out the river of His Spirit upon your children (and grandchildren):

_____

_____

_____

_____

_____

*T*hen I will sprinkle clean water on you, and you will be clean. I will take out your stony heart of sin and give you a new, obedient heart. And I will put my Spirit in you so you will obey my laws and do whatever I command (Ezek. 36:25–27).

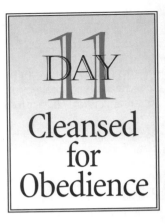

DAY 11

Cleansed for Obedience

To paraphrase a medieval story: A young monk came to the monastery's abbot wanting to learn obedience. So the abbot went into the abbey's orchard and snipped a cutting from one of the apple trees. Then he had the young monk carry a pail of water and follow him into the nearby desert.

After walking for about an hour, the abbot took the cutting and stuck it the ground. Then he poured water around the newly planted twig and told the monk, "Water this morning and evening until I tell you differently." So for three years, each morning and evening, the monk faithfully watered the apple cutting as it grew into a small tree. At the end of the three years, the abbot asked the monk, "Is there any fruit on your tree in the desert?"

"Yes, abbot," the young monk replied.

"Pick it and bring it to me," commanded the abbot.

So the young monk walked the mile out and back as he had done twice a day for three years. But this time he picked the fruit that had grown on his tree in the desert.

When he brought the apple to his abbot, the abbot instructed, "Now, eat the fruit of your obedience."

> *The river of God flows with the power to obey. We must exercise our will to obey, but the ability to obey comes from the Spirit of God.*

Paul in his strength lamented, "When I want to do good, I don't. And when I try not to do wrong, I do it anyway" (Rom. 8:19). But after he was indwelt by the Spirit, he declared, "For I can do everything with the help of Christ who gives me the strength I need" (Phil. 4:13).

What moved Paul from inadequacy and weakness to confidence and strength? Being born again by the faith in Jesus Christ.

List some of the problem areas in your life that you find most difficult to discipline into obedience in your own strength.

1. _____

2. _____

3. _____

4. _____

Since the river of God flows within you, you now have the power and ability to obey God. Read Jeremiah 31:33–34, and paraphrase it focusing on how God empowers you to obey Him:

_____

_____

_____

Ask yourself . . .

❖ How does the Holy Spirit empower you to trust and obey the Lord?

❖ When you disobey the Lord, what do you do?

Write a prayer thanking God for His Spirit flowing within you that empowers you to obey Him:

_____

_____

_____

_____

_____

I *will pour out my Spirit upon all peo-*
ple. Your sons and daughters will
prophesy. Your old men will dream
dreams. Your young men will see visions.
In those days, I will pour out my Spirit
even on servants, men and women alike
(Joel 2:28–29).

DAY 12

The Spirit Poured for Empowerment and Service

When the Spirit of God rains on us, we experience the supernatural. This pouring of the Spirit was fulfilled initially on the day of Pentecost in Acts 2.

Read Acts 2, then list the ways those baptized in the Holy Spirit encountered the supernatural power of God:

_____

_____

_____

_____

_____

Dreams occur when we sleep and visions appear when we are awake. God reveals Himself when we get out of the way. As *our* thoughts and actions are controlled by His Spirit, we become open and willing to receive *His* thoughts and actions.

Pentecost still happens when we are baptized and immersed in the river of God. Describe a time when you encountered Pentecost in your life.

_____

_____

The river of God is available to all—men and women—young and old. But the condition of receiving is a servant's heart.

In other words, humble and meek vessels are the ones God's river fills and indwells. How important is servanthood to encountering the river? Jot down what Jesus has to say about it:

Matthew 10:24 _____

Matthew 20:26–28 _____

Matthew 23:11 _____

Mark 10:43–45 _____

John 13:16 _____

The river of God flows through His servants to minister to others. God wants you to serve others so they can encounter His Spirit.

Ask yourself . . .

❖ In what ways is the Spirit empowering you to serve others?

❖ How are you encountering Pentecost today?

Write a prayer asking God to pour our His Spirit of Pentecost on you today:

_____

_____

_____

_____

_____

I baptize with water those who turn from their sins and turn to God. But someone is coming soon who is far greater than I am. . .He will baptize you with the Holy Spirit and with fire (Matt. 3:11).

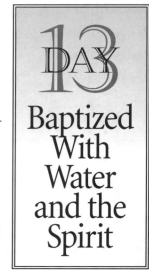

DAY 13
Baptized With Water and the Spirit

John's baptism in water for repentance foreshadowed Jesus' baptism in the Spirit and fire. When Jesus baptized in fire on Pentecost, a repentant people became an empowered people of God.

The river of God cleanses us from sin just as fire burns away all that is not pure and holy. Peter writes, "These trials are only to test your faith, to show that it is strong and pure. It is being tested as fire tests and purifies gold—and your faith is far more precious to God than mere gold" (1 Peter 1:7).

Have you experienced some trials in life that the Spirit has used to baptize you in fire? Describe one trial you have had that purified and cleansed your faith:

_____

_____

_____

Complete these sentences:

One area of my life that needs cleansing is _____

_____.

In order to yield totally to the Holy Spirit in this area of my life I need to _____

_____.

I will yield when _____

_____.

In repentance the river of God washes away our sin through the shed blood of Christ.

In Spirit baptism, the river of God flows through our lives with power and boldness to live the Christian life and minister with signs and wonders following.

Picture ocean waves as they wash upon the shore and flow back out to sea. Repentance is a spiritual wave that washes out the garbage of sin in our lives. The baptism of the Spirit washes in the abundance and gifts of God.

What garbage has the wave of repentance washed out of your life?

_____

_____

_____

What qualities and characteristics of the Spirit has the river of God washed into your life?

_____

_____

_____

Ask yourself . . .

❖ Have you fully yielded to the Holy Spirit?

❖ How is the river of God washing and cleansing your life?

Write a prayer asking Jesus to baptize you in His Spirit and fire:

_____

_____

_____

_____

_____

*A*fter his baptism, as Jesus came up out of the water, the heavens were opened and he saw the Spirit of God descending like a dove and settling on him. And a voice from heaven said, "This is my beloved Son, and I am fully pleased with him" (Matt. 3:16).

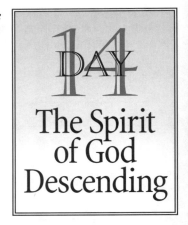

DAY 14
The Spirit of God Descending

At Jesus' baptism, two rivers were flowing—the natural river of the Jordan, and the spiritual river of God. In obedience, Jesus submitted Himself to baptism. For Him, baptism didn't follow repentance. Rather, Jesus was baptized to fulfill the will of His father.

Pleased with Jesus' obedience, the Father sent the Holy Spirit from heaven. This was the Son of God's moment of anointing and appointing to His ministry. Before this moment the Holy Spirit had indwelt Jesus, but He had not yet released Him into service. Now that the moment had come, the Spirit of God led Jesus into the wilderness to be tempted (Matt. 4:1) and then into a ministry empowered with miracles, signs, and wonders (Luke 4:14).

The example of Jesus' baptism teaches us much about the outpouring of the river of God. God's river is poured out from heaven when we are *obedient and totally submitted* to His will.

Are you obedient and submitted to God's will in each of the following areas of your life? Briefly describe your level of obedience in each category:

Ministry _____

Financial Matters _____

Marriage or Family _____

Work or Career _____

Relationships _____

The degree to which you are completely obedient and submitted to God's will in your life determines the degree to which the Spirit can work in your life.

> *When you are disobedient to God in an area of life, you shut off His river. But when you repent and become obedient in that area of your life, His river flows.*

Doing God's will is like turning the handle on a faucet that opens the flow of the Spirit's power. Read the following Scriptures, and jot down what they say about God's will:

Romans 12:1–1 _____

1 Peter 4:3 _____

1 John 2:15–17 _____

1 Thessalonians 4:3–5 _____

1 Thessalonians 5:12–22 _____

Ask yourself . . .

❖ What areas of your life are not yet fully submitted to the will of God?

❖ When will you repent and submit?

Write a prayer that completely surrenders every area of your life to the Lord:

_____

_____

_____

_____

_____

*B*ut when the Holy Spirit has come upon you, you will receive power and will tell people about me everywhere—in Jerusalem, throughout Judea, in Samaria, and to the ends of the earth (Acts 1:8).

Baptism means *to be immersed in water.* So how is one baptized in the Spirit? Where is the water? The water of Spirit baptism is the river of God that flows from His throne into our lives. His river produces a perpetual flow within us that fills us with the power and presence of God every moment of our lives.

You will receive power. Jesus promises that there is power in God's river. What power are you seeing evidenced in your life as a result of being immersed in His river? Is your life power-filled or powerless? Check all the evidences of Holy Spirit's power present now in your life:

❏ Signs and wonders   ❏ Holiness

❏ Gifts of the Spirit   ❏ Purity

❏ Hunger and thirst for God   ❏ Sharing with others

❏ Speaking in other languages   ❏ Love

❏ Deeper prayer, praises, and worship   ❏ Boldly witnessing

❏ Other: _____   ❏ Great joy and generosity

> *The river's power in your life empowers you to witness—*
> *sharing the good news of Jesus Christ with others.*

Are you a reluctant witness or a bold, empowered witness? Remember that the Holy Spirit will even give you the words you need when you witness (Luke 12:12). What keeps the power to witness shut off in your life? If you aren't witnessing boldly, check the things listed below that keep you from being a powerful witness:

❏ Fear   ❏ Embarrassment

❏ Ignorance   ❏ Too busy

❏ Disobedience   ❏ Not willing to get involved with unbelievers

❏ Other:_____

Ask yourself . . .

❖ What evidences of the river of God are you seeing in your life?

❖ With whom do you need to be sharing the gospel?

Write a prayer asking Jesus to baptize you in the river of God that fills your life with the power and presence of the Holy Spirit:

_____

_____

_____

_____

_____

*W*ell, I [Peter] began telling them [Cornelius' household] the Good News, but just as I was getting started, the Holy Spirit fell on them, just as he fell on us at the beginning (Acts 11:15).

DAY

Be Ready for the River

The household of Cornelius was ready for God's river to flow. They hadn't even heard a full presentation of the gospel when their river began to flow. In revivals across the centuries, evangelists would often simply stand up to preach and the Spirit of God would fall convicting and converting sinners. Why? The river of God flows when we are ready.

How did Cornelius and his household prepare themselves for the river? Before Peter even came to his house, Cornelius was preparing himself by giving and praying (Acts 10:2). In other words, Cornelius was doing everything within his own strength to seek God. The Word promises, "Draw close to God, and God will draw close to you" (James 4:8).

Read James 4:5–10. Notice how the Holy Spirit longs for our faithfulness and to draw us to Him. Below is a list of ways from James 4 that we may prepare ourselves to draw close to God. Check those you are presently doing, and circle those you need to start:

- ❑ Resisting evil desires
- ❑ Humbling ourselves
- ❑ Resisting the devil
- ❑ Coming clean before God through repentance and confession
- ❑ Being sorry for our sin
- ❑ Bowing down before God in worship and service
- ❑ Admitting our dependence upon Him
- ❑ Other: _____

Cornelius prepared himself and his household to meet God. Then God gave him a vision and Cornelius responded in obedience by sending a messenger to Peter. On Cornelius' part there was obedience and willingness to do whatever God commanded. Is there such willingness and obedience in your life?

The atmosphere in which the river of God flowed in Cornelius' house was charged with prayer, humility, obedience, and a desire for God to move.

And move He did! God poured out His river before Peter could even finish preaching. Are you prepared, and do you desire God's river as Cornelius did? Circle all the ways you need to draw near to God:

Prayer   Fasting   Service

Repentance   Worship   Praise

Study of the Word   Other:_____

Ask yourself . . .

❖ What are you doing to seek the river of God?

❖ In what areas of your life could your obedience and willingness increase?

Write a prayer that willingly seeks the river of God in your life:

_____

_____

_____

_____

_____

*D*on't you realize that all of you together are the temple of God and that the Spirit lives in you? (1 Cor. 3:16).

Wherever two or more believers gather together, Jesus is in their midst (Matt.18:20). So when we gather to worship and pray, that gathering becomes the temple, the church, over which Christ is the head. His presence in our midst is the Holy Spirit He sends to comfort, guide, teach, and counsel us.

Praise and prayer open the floodgates of the river of God as we gather together for worship. Streams and fountains flow within and out of us from the Spirit that form a tidal wave of His power and presence in our midst. Read Acts 2:33–47 and Acts 4:23–37. In a sentence describe how the river was released in the early church when they gathered together:

_____

_____

Now reflect upon your encounters with the Holy Spirit in worship, prayer, and praise with other believers. Complete the following sentences:

When we worship, we encounter_____

_____.

When we pray, we hear God's voice_____

_____.

When we praise, we sense the Holy Spirit_____

_____.

> *God delights in releasing His river upon His people as they worship, pray, and praise together.*

Not only is the river released corporately in the body of Christ, it also flows within us. Just as Ezekiel 47 and Revelation 22 describe the river and the temple, so 1 Corinthians 6:19 describes each believer as a temple of the Holy Spirit. The context of this passage speaks of the moral purity of the saint. The Spirit indwells pure vessels. Sexual immorality defiles the temple of the Holy Spirit and pollutes the river of God.

40

Examine your life, and answer each of the following questions with a *yes* or a *no*.

_____ I avoid looking at pornographic magazines and pictures.

_____ I refuse to view "sex" links on the Internet.

_____ I will not watch a movie, video, or television program that has sexually suggestive or explicit scenes.

_____ I will not listen to or speak sexually suggestive material or jokes.

_____ I resist looking upon the bodies of others with lust.

_____ I take unclean thoughts captive and rebuke them in the name of Jesus.

Ask yourself . . .

❖ How are you keeping your temple pure and unpolluted for the river of God?

❖ How is God's Spirit flowing through your worship?

Write a prayer of repentance that thanks God for keeping you pure from any sexual impurity in your life:

_____

_____

_____

_____

_____

*T*here was a time when some of you were just like that [living in sin], but now your sins have been washed away [or you have been cleansed], and you have been set apart for God (1 Cor. 6:11).

The river of God, the flow of His Holy Spirit, washes and cleanses you. Are there pollutants and dirt in your life that need to be washed away? Are you carrying around burdens of sin and guilt that need to be flushed out of your life? Then get into the river of God.

There is a story from the early days of exploring South America. A Portuguese sailing ship crossing the Atlantic was almost out of fresh water as she approached the South American coast. Still miles away from shore, the Portuguese captain spied another eastbound ship.

As the ships passed, he shouted to the other captain, "Can you spare some fresh water for us?"

"No, we have none to spare," the other captain shouted. But then he added, "Drop a bucket over the side."

Frustrated, the Portuguese captain shouted his request again, but the other ship was too far away by that time.

Confused, the thirsty captain had no option but to lower a bucket into the ocean. And when he did, it overflowed with pure, fresh, sweet water. He was in the flow of the Amazon. But what he didn't realize was that the fresh water pouring from the mouth of the Amazon remains fresh for miles out into the Atlantic before it finally becomes saturated with salt water.

In a parallel application, the flow of the river of God overcomes the salty, bitter flow of the world in our lives. Even though we are *in* the world, we are not *of* the world. Read 1 Corinthians 6:11. This passage describes what the flow of the Spirit in our lives does for us. After each statement, describe how the Spirit's flow has changed your life.

The Spirit . . .	**The change in me is . . .**
Cleanses (washes away sin)	_____
Sets us apart (sanctifies and makes holy)	_____
Makes us right with God (justifies and makes us righteous)	_____

The deepest change I have encountered in the river of God is _____

_____.

> *The more the Spirit's fresh water flows into your life, the less you will experience the polluted intrusion of the world's "salt" water.*

Ask yourself . . .

❖ What pollutants of sin do you need to have washed out of your life?

❖ How is the Holy Spirit justifying and sanctifying you today?

Write a prayer praising God for the refreshing waters of His Spirit that clean, wash, and purify your life:

_____

_____

_____

_____

_____

*T*he human body has many parts, but the many parts make up only one body. So it is with the body of Christ. Some of us are Jews, some are Gentiles, some are slaves, and some are free. But we have all been baptized into Christ's body by one Spirit, and we have all received the same Spirit (1 Cor. 12:12–13).

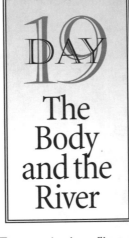

The Body and the River

The river of God brings unity to the body of Christ. All believers swim in the river. All drink of the same Spirit. And all are immersed by His living water.

So what causes the pollution of division to defile the body of Christ? Check the different pollutants you have observed trying to contaminate the church.

❑ Dissension ❑ Strife ❑ Unresolved conflict

❑ Rumors and gossip ❑ Pride ❑ Idolatry

❑ Prayerlessness ❑ False teaching ❑ Backbiting

❑ Offenses ❑ Backsliding ❑ Lack of vision

❑ Rebellion against authority ❑ Lack of commitment

❑ Compromising the truth of God's Word

❑ Disagreements over policy or money

❑ Other: _____

> *The Holy Spirit unifies His church.*

Maybe your church has been divided over issues of theology related to the Holy Spirit. Division can't be healed by compromise, votes, or discussion. It can only be healed by the Healer—Jesus Christ—who pours out the baptism of His Spirit upon His body. Prioritize the steps you believe your church needs to take to either remain in, or return to, the unity of the Holy Spirit:

_____ Repentance (Acts 2:38–42; 2 Cor. 7:8–11)

_____ Confession and fellowship (James 5:16–20; 1 John 1:5–10)

_____ Prayer (Eph. 5:15–20)

_____ Love (1 Cor. 13)

_____ Acceptance of weaker believers (Rom. 15:5–13)

_____ Forgiveness and reconciliation (Matt. 6:21–26; Eph. 2:11–18)

_____ Being humbled before God (James 4:5–17)

Ask yourself . . .

❖ What are you doing to flow in the unity of the Spirit in your church?

❖ How can you encourage the unity of the body when divisive elements arise in your church?

Write a prayer asking for the Holy Spirit's presence in bringing unity to the body of Christ:

_____

_____

_____

_____

_____

D *on't be drunk with wine, because that will ruin your life. Instead, let the Holy Spirit fill and control you (Eph. 5:18).*

One meaning of *being filled* with the Spirit of God is to be full to the top, so that all is completed, and there is no lack. When the river of God fills your life, God's power in you is sufficient to meet your every need and is able to meet every lack in your life.

Be Filled

Since the river of God fills our lives to overflowing in Christ, why do we experience lack? Listed below are some areas in the Christian life that at times may suffer lack. Put an *x* on the line where you are right now:

Finances

| Lack | Sufficient | Abundant |

Joy

| Lack | Sufficient | Abundant |

Peace

| Lack | Sufficient | Abundant |

Spiritual growth

| Lack | Sufficient | Abundant |

Faith

| Lack | Sufficient | Abundant |

Hope

| Lack | Sufficient | Abundant |

Love for enemies

| Lack | Sufficient | Abundant |

Discipline

| Lack | Sufficient | Abundant |

Patience

| Lack | Sufficient | Abundant |

Self-control

| Lack | Sufficient | Abundant |

Moral purity

| Lack | Sufficient | Abundant |

> *Lack never occurs because the Holy Spirit is unwilling or unable to pour out His river. His river's source is limitless and infinite.*

Rather, we lack because we:

❖ Don't ask (James 4:1–3).
❖ Ask with a doubtful mind (James 1:5–8).
❖ Seek things instead of the Spirit who possesses everything (Matt. 11:9–13).
❖ Harbor unforgiveness, which blocks God's forgiveness and power in us (Matt. 6:14–15).
❖ Hold onto broken relationships and offenses with others (Matt. 5:23–26).

Examine yourself. Is there a lack of filling in your life? If so, circle the reason(s) above you are experiencing it. Then repent to remove that area from your life.

The river of God meets and fills every need in our lives. We simply need to be filled with His Spirit.

Ask yourself . . .

❖ Are you being continually filled with the Spirit?

❖ What needs are being met by the river of God in your life?

❖ Is there anything blocking His filling in your life? If so, what is it, and will you repent?

Write a prayer asking Jesus to fill you with His Holy Spirit:

_____

_____

_____

_____

_____

*H*e saved us, not because of the good things we did, but because of his mercy. . .He generously poured out the Spirit upon us because of what Jesus Christ our Savior did (Titus 3:5–6).

The river of God is poured out generously upon our lives to bless us with God's mercy because of Jesus Christ.

How generous is God through Christ in pouring out His river? Below is a list of words that describe God's abundant and amazing grace in giving us His Spirit. Circle those that describe *for you* the depths of His grace:

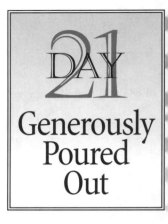

DAY 21

Generously Poured Out

Amazing	Abundant	Infinite
Undeserved	Free	Limitless
Lavish	Luxurious	Sufficient
Prodigious	Overflowing	

Other: _____

Why is the river of God given so generously? So we will have a limitless supply to share. One reason we tell others about the salvation of Jesus is because He has done so much for us. In addition to salvation, what has Jesus graciously done for you? Make a list.

1. _____

2. _____

3. _____

4. _____

Our response to the abundant, gracious gift of His river is to do deeds of kindness for everyone else—regardless of their ability to repay or thank us. Do indiscriminate acts of kindness!

Read Titus 3:8, then paraphrase the verse in your own words:

_____

_____

_____

Think of three people in your life to whom you are not usually gracious and kind. Now write down their names and what acts of kindness you will do for them in the coming week:

Name	Act of Kindness	When
_____	_____	_____
_____	_____	_____
_____	_____	_____

Ask yourself . . .

❖ What are you doing to try to *earn* His grace that you need to surrender?

❖ In what ways are you now showing gratitude to God for His grace?

Write a prayer thanking God for His amazing grace in pouring out His river on you:

_____

_____

_____

_____

_____

*S*o we have these three witnesses—the Spirit, the water, and the blood—and all three agree (1 John 5:7).

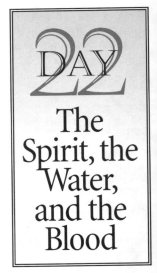

DAY 22

The Spirit, the Water, and the Blood

How can we know for certain that Jesus was the Christ, the Son of God, and that through Him we are saved and filled with the river of His Spirit? Three witnesses assure us.

1. *The Water.* At Jesus' baptism, God anointed Him with the Spirit and proclaimed for all to see and hear that Jesus was His Son (Mark 1:9–11; Luke 3:21–22; John 1:31–34).

2. *The Blood.* Jesus' shed blood and death on the cross cleanses us from sin. He paid the price of our guilt and washes us white as snow with His blood (Isa. 1:18; Rom. 5:6–11).

3. *The Spirit.* The Holy Spirit breathed on Jesus' disciples after His resurrection (John 20:22) and poured out upon His followers at Pentecost (Acts 2) confirms Jesus as Lord and Savior.

These three witnesses are also at work in your life. They stream through you in God's river flowing with the Spirit's new life, healing, cleansing, and refreshing. Describe what these witnesses mean to you:

Baptism witnesses in my life the truth that _____

_____.

The blood of Jesus _____

_____.

The Holy Spirit assures me _____

_____.

Survey after survey confirms that a vast majority of Americans believe Jesus is the Christ. But only about half of those really accept the sacrifice of His shed blood for the remission of their sins. Some mystics and religious seekers are even willing to accept that Jesus came as a great spiritual teacher. But they are unwilling to acknowledge that Jesus is the Son of Man, who suffered and died for the sins of the world on the cross. Look up each of the following passages that speak about the cross and the blood of Christ. Then write down what each of them says about salvation.

Matthew 26:28; Mark 14:24 _____

Romans 3:25 _____

Romans 5:8; 7:4 _____

1 Corinthians 1:17–18; 2:2 _____

Galatians 3:1, 13; 5:11; 6:12 _____

Ephesians 1:7 _____

Colossians 1:14 _____

> *The river of God's Spirit transforms us into fountains of living water from which others may drink of the Good News and encounter our witness of Jesus' saving grace through His Spirit, blood, and water.*

Ask yourself . . .

❖ How does the shed blood of Christ witness through your life of His grace and salvation?

❖ Who needs to drink from the river flowing through you?

Write a prayer thanking God for the witness of the water, blood, and Spirit in your life:

_____

_____

_____

_____

_____

A river brings joy to the city of our God, the sacred home of the Most High (Ps. 46:4).

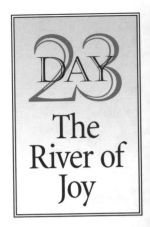

Day 23

The River of Joy

Sad-faced Christians who live from crisis to crisis are cut off from the flow of God's river. They have allowed the circumstances of life to overflow them.

Jesus, the man of sorrows (Isa. 53:3), was filled with the joy of the Holy Spirit. Because of our Lord, the river of God brings into our inner selves an abiding joy that can't be stolen or robbed, no matter what our circumstances (John 16:16–33).

To discover the depth of joy that comes through a living relationship with God, read each of the following passages and jot down a summary of what it reveals about joy:

1 Chronicles 16:10 _____

Psalm 4:7–8 _____

Psalm 9:1–2 _____

Psalm 16:11 _____

Psalm 30:5–11 _____

Psalm 68:4 _____

Psalm 118:24 _____

Isaiah 61:3–10 _____

Jude 1:24 _____

The flow of the Spirit brings continual joy and blessings into our lives. Wherever the presence of the Lord is. . .wherever the river of God flows. . .there is joy! Jesus declares in John 16 that nothing can overcome or steal your joy. So when some say the devil has stolen their joy, they must be mistaken. Because the devil, the world, circumstances, or enemies, can never steal our joy. Rather, some willfully and tragically lose their joy when they separate themselves from the Holy Spirit's presence through sin, rebellion, and pride.

What is it that shuts off God's river of joy in your life? Check those things that most often tempt you to let go of your joy in the Lord.

❑ Pride   ❑ Discouragement

❑ Fear   ❑ Anxiety

- ❏ Anger
- ❏ Failure
- ❏ Other: _____

- ❏ Depression
- ❏ Unfulfilled expectations

> *Joy comes in the river. So don't give it away or allow anything to take it. Nothing can steal your joy. Only you can lose it.*

Ask yourself . . .

❖ For *what* and *when* do you rejoice in the Holy Spirit?

❖ What do you need to do to keep from losing your joy?

Write a prayer that rejoices in the Lord:

_____

_____

_____

_____

_____

*W*hen the poor and needy search for water and there is none. . .then I, the Lord, will answer them. . .I will open up rivers. . .I will give them fountains of water in the valleys. In the deserts they will find pools of water. Rivers fed by springs will flow across the dry, parched ground (Isa. 41:17–19).

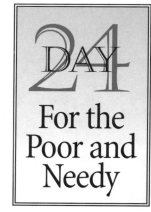

For the Poor and Needy

Those who thirst for the river of God will be given fountains of waters. Jesus declared that "God blesses those who realize their need for him, for the kingdom of God is given to them" (Matt. 5:3). Especially the poor and needy.

God makes a tremendous promise to the poor and needy. He says His river will flow across their deserts and parched land, forming pools of living waters. So, those who recognize their spiritual poverty and desperate need for God will ultimately find Him and have their thirst quenched.

Complete the following sentences:

From the river of God, I thirst most for_____

_____.

From the river of God, I most need_____

_____.

What we often believe we need most in life is that which we need the least. For example, we may believe in times of financial crisis that what we need is money. But our real thirst in times of need can only be satisfied by the Spirit of wisdom who teaches us how to manage the money we have. So, we often want the very opposite of what we truly hunger for and need.

Think of the following opposites which are true needs that can only be met by the river of God's Holy Spirit:

We want vengeance. . .but we need _____.

We want to be justified. . .but we need _____.

We want money. . .but we need _____.

We want prosperity. . .but we need _____.

We want to be first. . .but we need _____.

We want to be served. . .but we need _____.

We want pleasure. . .but we need _____.

When in the desert, we may think we need to escape the wilderness to end our suffering. But what we truly need is living water from God that will make it possible to live in the desert and endure the heat.

> *When you are in the desert, don't look to escape. Look for God's river to quench your thirst and satisfy your deepest need.*

Ask yourself . . .

❖ What do I truly need most from the river of God?

❖ What praises do I need to raise in thanksgiving to the Spirit for satisfying my deepest thirst and needs?

Write a prayer asking the Lord for your needs—not your wants:

_____

_____

_____

_____

_____

*T*hey are like trees planted along the riverbank,
bearing fruit each season without fail. Their
leaves never wither, and in all they do, they
prosper (Ps. 1:3).

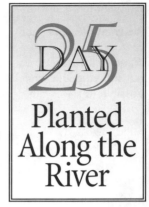

Those who don't follow the advice of the wicked,
stand around with sinners, or join in with scoffers
are like trees planted by the river of God. Those
who draw nourishment from the river of God's Spirit
aren't fed by the negative, critical sewers of the
world. So God's river is to flow unceasingly in and
through us, and we must guard our hearts against
all that would pollute us.

The first pollutant is *the advice of the wicked*. Below is a listing of the types of
advice the wicked give. Prioritize from 1 (most likely to tempt me), to 6 (least
likely to tempt me).

_____ "You should never trust anyone."

_____ "Look out for #1."

_____ "The end justifies the means."

_____ "Success depends completely on you."

_____ "Don't get mad, get even."

_____ "If it feels good do it."

> *An important attribute of prosperous people is
> their intolerance of godlessness. You will become
> like those with whom you build relationships.*

A second pollutant is *standing around with sinners*. Your friends will either fill
you with life, or fill you with death. It is much easier for sinners to pull you
down than for you to pull them up. So the less you associate with some people, the more your life will improve.

List the three people with whom you spend the most time, and put an *x* on
the line that describes their lives:

Name

1._____   _____

                              Ungodly   Godly

2. _____

                     Ungodly   _____   Godly

3. _____

                     Ungodly   _____   Godly

A third pollutant that can contaminate God's will in our lives is *joining in with negative, critical scoffers* who always blame others for their problems. When they can't find another person to blame, they blame God. Have you ever done any of this? Do you ever scoff? Do an attitude check. Circle any of the following qualities of a scoffer that you may have:

Negative	Critical	Judgmental
Cynical	Angry	Vengeful
Pessimistic	Distrustful	Paranoid

Other: _____

Finally, the benefits of being planted along God's riverbank include the bearing of His spiritual fruit (Gal. 5:22–23), and prospering in all you do (Ps. 37:1–5).

Ask yourself . . .

❖ Which of my friends may be polluting any area of my life?

❖ What good fruit is my life bearing?

❖ How is the Spirit prospering my life?

Write a prayer asking God for a continual hunger for His Word, day and night:

_____

_____

_____

_____

_____

*A*s the deer pants for streams of water, so I long for you, O God. I thirst for God, the living God. When can I come and stand before Him? (Ps. 42:1–2).

Thirst becomes a daily need for everyone who drinks from the river of God. Just as water is essential for physical life, living water is an absolute necessity for our spiritual well-being.

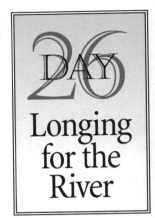

Longing for the River

> *Thirsting for God makes you desperately needful of all that His river has for you.*

Prioritize from 1 (most thirsty), to 12 (least thirsty).

I thirst for . . .

_____ His presence

_____ His glory

_____ His love

_____ His communion

_____ His righteousness

_____ His holiness

_____ His Word

_____ His peace

_____ His salvation

_____ His power

_____ His grace

_____ His purity

The river of God leads you directly to Jesus. "When the Spirit of truth comes, he will guide you into all truth. He will not be presenting his own ideas; he will be telling you what he has heard. He will tell you about the future. He will bring me [Jesus] glory by revealing to you whatever he receives from me. All that the Father has is mine; this is what I mean when I say that the Spirit will reveal to you whatever he receives from me" (John 16:13–15).

What is the Spirit revealing to you about Jesus? Briefly describe what He is teaching you now:

_____

_____

_____

_____

The more we drink from the river of God, the more we thirst for Him. We can never drink enough. Though satisfied for a moment, we quickly grow thirsty again for more and more of His water. That is how we grow deeper and deeper in the Spirit—drinking from the river of God.

Ask yourself . . .

❖ In what way is my thirst for God's river increasing?

❖ How am I satisfying my thirst for His river? (i.e. prayer, study of the Word, worship, praise, etc.)

Write a prayer that asks God to daily increase your thirst for His river:

_____

_____

_____

_____

_____

A nd when he [the Redeemer] comes. . .Springs will gush forth in the wilderness, and streams will water the desert. The parched ground will become a pool, and springs of water will satisfy the thirsty land. . .Sorrow and mourning will disappear, and they [the redeemed] will be overcome with joy and gladness (Isa. 35:5–7, 10).

Springs Will Gush Forth

The evidence of God's river is all around us. When His river flows in our midst, wonderful things happen. God's glory and splendor are displayed. The sick are healed. Those who are hungry and thirsty for the Spirit are filled. Holiness becomes the way of life. The enemies of God flee. And joy washes away sorrow.

Are you encountering the move of the Holy Spirit in any of these ways? Below is a list of some of the ways the river of God flows through His people as revealed in Isaiah 35. Check His ways you are currently encountering, and circle the ways that you thirst for the most.

❏ Rejoicing, joy, gladness, and laughter

❏ The glory of God

❏ Encouragement

❏ Healing

❏ Good news from His Word

❏ Holiness

❏ Redemption

❏ Renewing

❏ Living water for those in the desert

❏ Strength

❏ Salvation

❏ Singing

❏ Abundance

❏ Victory over the enemies of God

❏ Restoration

❏ Songs of everlasting joy

The river of God is a highway of holiness. Just as rivers are used in many parts of the world as major highways for transporting people and commerce, so God's river transports the things of heaven to earth.

> *God's river carries His presence and Spirit from His throne into, and through, our lives.*

Ask yourself . . .

❖ How are you encountering the manifestations of God's river in your life and church?

❖ What is your greatest joy in God's river?

Write a prayer asking God to daily increase your thirst for His river:

_____

_____

_____

_____

_____

F or I [the Lord] am about to do a brand-new thing. See, I have already begun! Do you not see it? I will make a pathway through the wilderness for my people to come home. I will create rivers for them in the desert (Isa. 43:18–19).

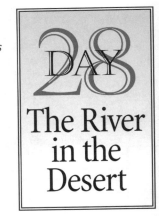

DAY 28

The River in the Desert

Some people seem to prefer deserts to rivers. Why is that? Fear! Those who haven't learned to swim often fear the water. And swimming (not just wading) is a new experience to any who hate whatever is new, changing, and fresh.

God's river always transforms our deserts. Deserts are the old patterns, habits, sins, and bondages in our lives. The river of God washes away the old and brings in new life, with changed behaviors and attitudes, and fresh new ways to worship and minister. While traditions teach, instruct, and encourage, they should never stifle, block, or hinder the new and refreshing flow of God's river.

Below are some passages that reveal the newness of God in our lives. Read each Scripture and jot down the new things of His Spirit that He makes available in our lives:

2 Corinthians 5:17 _____

Psalm 96:1; 98:1 _____

Isaiah 11:1–10 _____

Isaiah 40:31 _____

Isaiah 42:16 _____

Isaiah 48:6–8 _____

Matthew 9:17 _____

Mark 16:7 _____

John 3:6 _____

Romans 5:11 _____

Romans 7:6 _____

2 Corinthians 3:6–12 _____

Galatians 6:15 _____

Are you resisting the new things of God's Spirit that He wants to flow into your life? If you are, ask yourself now why you are resisting. Then circle any of the following attitudes that may be blocking His flow in your life:

Fear	Dislike change
Tradition	Lack of confidence
Unbelief	Other: _____

Whatever new thing God has for us is transported in His river. It is watered and nourished by His Spirit. Then it is empowered and happens through the strength of His Spirit. It doesn't depend on your ability. It depends on your availability.

Ask yourself . . .

❖ What new thing is the river of God producing in your life?

❖ What needs to be overcome within you so you won't resist the new things of God?

Write a prayer asking God to create, by His Spirit, whatever new thing He desires in your life:

_____

_____

_____

_____

_____

A Rock, and water gushed out to form a river through the dry and barren land (Ps. 105:41).

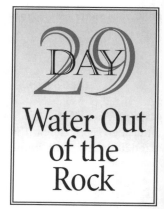

DAY 29

Water Out of the Rock

As God led Israel through the wilderness, He provided for every need that His people had, including, food, shelter, clothing, water, protection, and health.

As we go through the deserts and wildernesses of our own lives, God does the same for us. The living water of God flows from out of His rock. So what's His rock? Find out for yourself. Read the following passages and jot down what you learn:

The Text	The Rock is. . .
Psalm 18:2, 46	
Psalm 19:14	
Psalm 28:1	
Psalm 62:2–3	
Psalm 78:16, 20	
Isaiah 26:4	
Isaiah 44:8	
Matthew 7:24-25	
Luke 20:17–18	
1 Peter 2:6–8	

> *Out of Jesus, the Rock of our salvation, flows God's living water—the river of His Spirit.*

The Rock of our salvation gives us a firm foundation to make the solid decisions necessary when withstanding the storms and attacks of the world.

How has His Spirit helped you stand firm on the Rock of Christ? Write all the ways on the rock below.

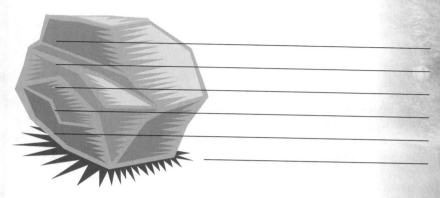

_____
_____
_____
_____
_____
_____

Ask yourself . . .

❖ When do you need living water from the Rock the most in your daily walk?

❖ What battle do you face the most that requires you to stand firm on the Rock and drink of His water?

Write a prayer asking God to flow His river from the Rock of Christ into your life:

_____
_____
_____
_____
_____

I *f you sinful people know how to give good gifts*
to your children, how much more will your
heavenly Father give the Holy Spirit to those
who ask him? (Luke 11:13).

DAY 30

Drink
Deeply
From the
River of
God

Finally, in this study, the river of God is yours only
for the asking. The Father greatly desires to give
you the fullness of His river as you repent of sin
and ask in faith. Only your sin and pride can
hinder the river's flow.

So die to self (Gal. 2:20). Decide to let God's
river flow unimpeded in and through your life. If
there are impeding factors restricting God's full
flow, complete the following sentences to single
them out:

What hinders the river in my life is _____

_____

_____.

What I need to repent of is _____

_____.

One way I repeatedly get in the way of God is_____

_____.

The thing in self I need to die to is _____

_____.

Now take a moment to reflect on how you've encountered the Holy Spirit over
the past thirty days. Complete the following sentences:

My most important revelation about the Holy Spirit has been _____

_____.

One way the Spirit is doing a deeper work in my life is _____

_____.

My thirst for God's river has _____

_____.

My desire to swim in God's river is _____

_____.

The new thing that the Holy Spirit is doing in my life is _____

_____ .

Remember:

> *Your yieldedness to the Holy Spirit determines*
> *the flow of His river into your life.*

Ask yourself . . .

❖ What needs to be surrendered in my life to increase the flow of His river?

❖ How willing am I to share His living water with others?

Write a prayer that thanks Jesus for sending the river of His Spirit to flow in
and through your life:

_____

_____

_____

_____

_____

> You can continue your encounters with the Holy Spirit by using the
> other devotional study guides listed at the end of this booklet, and
> by using the companion *Holy Spirit Encounter Bible.*

Leader's Guide

For Group Sessions

This devotional study is an excellent resource for group study including such settings as:

❖ Sunday school classes and other church classes
❖ Prayer groups
❖ Bible study groups
❖ Ministries involving small groups, home groups, and accountability groups
❖ Study groups for youth and adults

Before the First Session

❖ Contact everyone interested in participating in your group to inform them about the meeting time, date, and place.
❖ Make certain that everyone has a copy of this devotional study guide.
❖ Plan out all your teaching lessons before starting the first session. Also ask group members to begin their daily encounters in this guide. While each session will not strictly adhere to a seven-day schedule, group members who faithfully study a devotional every day will be prepared to share in the group sessions.
❖ Pray for the Holy Spirit to guide, teach, and help each participant.
❖ Be certain the place where you meet has a chalkboard, white board, or flipchart with appropriate writing materials.

Planning the Group Sessions

1. You will have four sessions together as a group. So plan to cover at least seven days in each session. If your sessions are weekly, then have your group complete the final two days prior to your last session.

2. In your first session, have group members find a partner with whom they will share and pray each time you meet. Keep the same pairs throughout the group sessions. See if you can randomly put pairs together—men with men, and women with women.

3. Have group and class members complete their devotional studies prior to their group sessions to enhance group sharing, study, and prayer. Begin each session with prayer.

4. Either the group leader or selected members should read the key Scriptures from each of the seven daily devotionals you will be studying in the session.

5. As the leader, you should decide which exercises and questions are to be covered prior to each session.

6. Also decide which exercises and sessions will be most appropriate to share with the group as a whole, or in pairs.

7. Decide which prayer(s) from the seven devotionals you will want the pairs to pray with one another.

8. Close each session by giving every group member the opportunity to share with the group how he or she encountered the Holy Spirit during the previous week. Then lead the group in prayer or have group members pray aloud in a prayer circle as you close the session.

9. You will have nine days of devotionals to study in the last session. So, use the last day as an in-depth sharing time in pairs. Invite all the group members to share the most important thing they learned about the Holy Spirit during this study and how their relationship with the Spirit was deepened because of it. Close with prayers of praise and thanksgiving.

10. Remember to allow each person the freedom "not to share" with their prayer partner or in public if they are uncomfortable with it.

11. Always start and end each group session on time and seek to keep them no longer than ninety minutes.

12. Finally, be careful. This is not a therapy group. Group members who seek to dominate group discussions with their own problems or questions should be ministered to by the group leader or pastor one on one outside of the group session.

Titles in the Holy Spirit Encounter Guide Series

Additional Notes

Additional Notes

Additional Notes

Additional Notes

Additional Notes

Additional Notes

Additional Notes

Additional Notes

Additional Notes

Additional Notes